WHAT THINGS ARE MADE OF

PITT POETRY SERIES

Ed Ochester, Editor

WHAT THINGS ARE MADE OF

CHARLES HARPER WEBB

University of Pittsburgh Press

Published by the University of Pittsburgh Press, Pittsburgh, Pa., 15260
Copyright © 2013, Charles Harper Webb
All rights reserved
Manufactured in the United States of America
Printed on acid-free paper
10 9 8 7 6 5 4 3 2 1

ISBN 13: 978-0-8229-6229-8
ISBN 10: 0-8229-6229-2

for Karen and Erik

CONTENTS 3 SECTIONS— PAST, PRESENT, FUTURE

I

II

III

WHAT THINGS ARE MADE OF

PART I

making fun of literary elements.

Nostalgia's Not What It Used To Be

I'm well aware it's problematic to miss the ice cream trucks
that clinked and tinkled down Candlelight Lane. The name
"Good Humor" privileged bourgeois affability, and valorized
consumption. Songs the trucks played—"Daisy, Daisy"
and "Dixie"—legitimized patriarchy, women's oppression,
and the Mariana Trench of slavery. My memory of Sterling

Roig, Bobbi Jo Smith, Carol Kamas, Clarkie Lauderdale
blasting from houses, clutching dimes and clamoring,
present as *facts*, subjective impressions of *friends* who may
have cared nothing for me, or cared because of under-
theorized notions of *neighborhood* and *kinship-of-the-same*.
The products sold reinforced a Capitalist hegemony—

Fudgesicle (racist), Eskimo (not Inuit) Pies, Torpedo
(military-industrial imperialist), Popsicle (no Momsicle), etc.
The sugar in our treats deconstructed sweetness into cavities,
obesity, diabetes. The (always) man in (always) white—
who pulled, from the back of his condensation-smoking-truck,
products iced with polluted air which our tongues melted,

loving the cold jolt—may have been a child-molester,
exploited immigrant, or untreated dyslexic. What I remember
as a smile, a laugh like Santa's, could have been a sneer,
leer, or consumptive hack. The bond of signifier/signified,
which I thought solid as Galveston's seawall,
was slithery as New York City slush. No one involved

understood anyone else, which explains the time I asked
for a red Torpedo, and got green. Red, by the way, evokes
strawberry (a bruise), and farting *raspberries*, as well
as Communism, which evokes the rapacious USA, its sacred texts
indeterminate as the location of electrons in a quantum world
where "truth" shifts like ants on the Klondike (raped

3

environment) Bar I dropped, so the vendor gave me (liberated
from his corporate slave-master) another one. Maybe
he cursed me covertly as the spoiled spawn of world-despoilers.
Still, I picture how he climbed back in his truck, waved,
and drove off, grinning, as dusk sifted gently down,
while we exploiters of the proletariat, bellies stuffed with Mom's

counter-revolutionary cooking, licked our pelf, and resumed
our games of jump-rope, doctor, Who's the Prettiest?,
or Grand Slam, and on the last pitch of the day, I sent the ball
sailing over Clarkie's house, through the warm suburban dark
into a black-hole future that had been always already sucking
what I thought was happiness away.

Where Are You Now, Sally Woodman,

who won the spelling bee with *centrifugal*—
who sang in church choir, and brought the most canned
goods for starving Africans? You sat behind me
from second to sixth grade, let me use your scissors

when mine broke, tore pages from your notebook
when I left mine home, and when you had three Oreos,
gave me two. Where are you, Sally, who hand-
picked my Valentine, while I pulled yours

from the Value Pac Mom bought for the whole class?
Where is your bobbed blonde hair, your eyes'
morning-glory blue, your skin—*porcelain*
Mom called it—that burned pink if I said "Hi"?

Where are you, fresh and cheerful as the Holsum Maid
on our milk boxes—much better for me
than Kimi Kidsen, I saw clearly when she gave back
my dog tag, and I whiffed three times in a playoff game—

better by miles than Candy Sanders, who swished
her ponytail and wiggled hips as straight as mine,
scattering smiles like pink balloons among the boys.
When, shaking worse than with the flu, I gasped,

"Will you be my May Fete partner? Please?"
Candy chirped, "I'm sorry—Tommy asked first,"
meaning Tommy Tucker, who couldn't keep a beat
if it was welded to his head, let alone sing for his supper,

but rode his chopped Ducati in high hoodlum style.
Back I dragged to my sad desk, where Sally—blue
eyes cast down—must have seen my spilled guts coiling
on the ground, must have known I knew she'd be

my partner if I asked her to. "Why can't you love
what's good for you?" I call down through the cruel years,
and hear my voice from way back then call, "Why
can't *you?*"

Vitus & Me

I was no saint,
God knew; but I suffered through church to please
my mom, preaching to myself, "Sit still, sit still."
I scourged myself with school, forcing my face
into the chloroform of names, dates, conjugations
while my toes writhed, buried alive in my shoes.
Better that
than being racked, as Vitus was. Still, in my torment,
I imagined guardian angels: herky-jerky
Lew Burdette of the Braves; the bouncy boppers
on American Bandstand, where "Itchy Twitchy
Feeling" was my favorite song.
My parents promised

ADHD?

age would cure my fidgets; they were wrong.
Even now, my pulse shouts down the calm lyric,
and blasts me toward the comic rhapsody, the frenzied
psalm. That's *my* seat squeaking at the movies,
my head bouncing like a speed-bag as everyone
behind me fights to see.
"It's energy," I told Dad,
"Christ!" he said, and didn't understand.
How much
of Christ could the brightest eight-year-old understand?
Vitus—senator's son raised by Christian slaves—
was torn apart for parroting what those he loved
like parents made him say. (I'll bet they promised him
no pain.)

*Not fitting in
Not belonging
or being true
to self.*

St. Valentine's dance became a celebration
in the vain, panting dark of high school gyms.
Vitus's became a disease.
At a play I paid a hundred bucks
to see, I'm about to twitch out of my skin
till I observe, behind me, a woman's crossed leg
jigging crazily. Just one blue button keeps
her skirt from splitting open past her knee.

She smiles, seeing that I see. A billion sperm start
wriggling.

        As we lie, later, in each other's arms,
the state of grace poor Vitus died for, falls on us

                              for free.

The best stuff in life is free.

Dark Penguin

After the oil spill, he's front-page news: a beak-faced,
heart-sick Muppet who *fell into a vat of chocolate,*
as the Lowes Bros sang to packed houses in the fifties,
before so-called folk music fell from grace.
Folks had more substantial molecules back then.

You could still meet an old black man cane-poling,
and he'd call you *Son,* and knock you flat in the mud
with catfish wisdom. But *Dem days done gone.*
Feathered and tarred, our penguin looks depressed
enough for shock therapy. Those scientists who say

only humans feel emotion, never owned a dog,
a vindictive ferret, or ambivalent lovebird. They're no
Einsteins, those scientists. Albert and Tammy Tortoise
were a happy pair before a neighbor gave me
a new female: younger than Tammy, more lineated shell,

a chelonian hard-body, which Al banged right away.
(They really banged, shell against shell. Day after day.)
Tammy took to her burrow, and died. My grandma
died when Mom was nine. Death didn't hide in hospitals
back then. Folk was the only music on the farm

where Grandma squeezed out her eight kids—three dead
before cancer killed her at thirty-five. Mom watched her fall
in on herself like a cardboard box in flames.
The sight hardened: a lump of fear she passed to me
like an heirloom that Goodwill can never haul away,

and no matter where you dump it, drags back home.
Dick Lowes won't let his son come home since Dick Jr.
played Taylor Bust in a porn film and made his mother cry.
Mr. July, the Eastern Box on my *World Turtles* calendar,
has an orange-spotted shell and crimson eyes like Torpy T,

crushed by a truck when I was ten. I cried that day
the way I want to when July ends, and a Hawksbill—
endangered—takes poor Torpy's place. Dark Penguin,
if it lives, will pass on its dark fears: orcas, great whites,
gooey black seas. The days of virgin ice and endless

krill have gone the way of folk songs and *Dragnet*.
I'd forgotten that show until, last night, an owl called
Who-hoo-*who*-hoo like the theme. So long, Sergeant Friday.
So long, "Just the facts, ma'am." So long, husband
of my friend Mary Ann, who stays in her burrow and cries.

In water, flightless penguins fly. They range in size
from emperor (4 feet, 90 pounds) to fairy (16 inches, 2 pounds).
The newspapers don't tell the species of their cover-bird.
Maybe its bird-brain had no hopes to crush and grind.
Maybe its sorrow's all in the beholder's mind.

Mummies To Burn

During a railway expansion in Egypt in the nineteenth century,
construction companies unearthed so many mummies that they
used them as locomotive fuel.

—*Discover Magazine*

The companies didn't think of *ka*s whimpering
as the bodies where they'd meant to spend eternity
dispersed in desert wind. Nor did the companies care

how many children weren't conceived
when workmen woke, shuddering, at night,
confusing their wives with the desecrated dead—

the gaping mouths; the yellow, glaring teeth;
the mummy stink. These were not days (except
in print) for tender sensibilities. Mobs howled

for hangings. Corpses cluttered the streets
in that time of White Man's Burden—of Drag
the Wogs to Western Ways, and Make Them Pay.

So to the flames the mummies went. Earth
spewed them forth, plentiful as passenger pigeons,
common as the cod that clogged Atlantic seas.

No fear the supply would ever end. No need
to save for tomorrow mummies abundant as air,
mummies good for turning water into steam

to drive the great iron trains that dragged
behind them, in an endless chain of black, shrieking cars,
the Modern Age.

News of Him

Filming for Pepsi, he hip-hops down a flight
        of golden stairs. A Roman candle, spraying colors
                like a feather headdress, strokes his hair,

which flares into a crown of flames. That day
        his surgeries begin: nose turned up cute as a girl's;
                cheeks lifted; eyes widened; lips thinned;

black skin bleached tan, then angel-white.
        The voice, high and pure as an angel's, doesn't
                change. Nor does he use it to blow critics

into The Pit—only to build Neverland, where kids ride
        Ferris wheels, scarf candy, patty-cake with chimps,
                and—in a swimming-pool-sized bed, on pillows

puffed like clouds, and smooth, winter-white
        sheets—join him in (he swears) innocent sleep.
                Naturally, persecution comes: search warrants,

lawsuits, exposés, then mocking, scourging,
        settling out of court, along with plunging record
                sales, botched marriages, his bone-white children

veiled as he retreats behind the mask of sorrow
        all gods know. Multitudes hear a doctor on TV
                describe their savior's *end-stage* nose.

A black Judas betrays him on the BBC. The press
        crucifies him, and he weeps—not for himself,
                for *them,* his followers say. For he so loved

the world, he gave it the moonwalk and *Thriller.*
        He preached the gospel of "Black or White,"
                and "Beat It." He showed how *bad* was good,

advised us to be *startin' somethin'*, and not
  to stop till we got enough. He promised never
    to grow old as he appeared, hearing *Not Guilty*.

Now, as war's atomic lizard flames up from the sea,
  and we buy duct tape to seal out toxic air,
    we fill deflated lives with news of him.

Remembering the boy who sang "I'll Be There,"
  "I Want You Back," and "Never Can Say Goodbye,"
    we watch him descend, again and again,

the golden stairs, bringing his message of hope
  and joy and Pepsi-Cola, his hair flaming
    with celestial light.

Jackass: The Viewer

Why do I remember *Jackass: The Movie* when so much
has gushed from the cracked crankcase of my mind?
My brain has dumped the words King Lear howled

on the heath, but saved the Fool promising some car-
rental guy, "I'll take good care of this baby," then racing
straight to Demolition Derby. I can't remember women

I've slept with, or forget Sir Wastebasket-Head pedaling
his bike through a grocery store, push-broom lance scattering
canned goods as he falls. I can't define *Bauhaus*,

but recall the industrial-strength moron who paper-cut
his own tongue, then—shot with a bean-bag gun—screamed,
wriggled, writhed on the floor, and later showed off

a black-and-purple bruise big as a fist. Paying the phone bill
slips my mind, but not "Bungee Jump Wedgie."
Brains hold tight to what they think helps them survive—

not Nobel Prize economics, but "Ass Kicked by a [Karate
Champion] Girl." Not my anniversary, or St. Thomas's
thoughts on teleology, but air-horns sqwonking as pro

golfers flail. I barely smile watching that French mime
What's-His-Name, but nearly fill my pantaloons
when a guy cracks a newspaper in a hardware store,

then deflowers the display commode. I've fuzzed the year
of William's conquest, but see clearly Wee Man—
four-foot-none—high-kicking his own head, then strolling,

hidden under a red traffic cone, as heedless crowds surge by.
Why is High Culture so hard to grasp today?
Why is History so easily displaced? Is my life a waste

because I can't recite the periodic table, or Boyle's law,
or the first bars of Beethoven's Ninth, or my password
to the *Times* online archives, or how many cups

in a gallon, or my city councilman (if I have one),
or my state senator or national representative, or how
to take square roots, or who won the Battle of Bull Run,

or the difference between Lope de Vega and Cabeza
de Vaca, or exactly why my ex filed on me,
but I remember the white guy in Tokyo who snorted hot

wasabi until he threw up. His fellow diners seemed
incredulous at first, then laughed so hard that one bent down
and threw up too.

why does it always seem like we forget the important stuff, but can always remember the dumb stuff?

Everybody Tries So Hard

And every *thing*: the squirrels that have plenty of nuts,
but keep on packing their fat cheeks, saving, saving—
the pigeons that flap so hard to get their corn-fed bodies
off the ground when Timmy runs up with his dog,
trying for a mouthful of feathers, a handful of flight.

The steel propellers in Cheeseburger Delight's silver cans
spin like mad to mix ice cream, chocolate, and milk
into a malt human livers bust their trusses to digest,
the drinkers straining to believe they're still wasp-waisted,
seventeen, life opening like a field of golden poppies

in the sky. It infarcts my heart how hard they try—
like the man, sweat on his pate, buttocks pumping
as he puffs, "I think I can," his partner straining, eyes
squinched shut in what (good worker!) she hopes is ecstasy—
like convicts who swill their putrid jail-brewed Pruno,

trying to rouse a decent drunk while thousands of breast-
feeding moms march, trying so hard to upset the government—
panting, lugging babies furrow-faced with concentration,
frantic to feed brains that will spend their lives trying
to get ahead like those farmers who broke their backs

growing tobacco until the court's indignant klieg light
turned on them, hundreds of lawyers, rubbed raw
by law school, trying so hard to make their hard
trying pay. As writs, statutes, subpoenas dropped
like stogie-chomping locusts on the fields of Marlboro

and Pall Mall, the farmers fought to keep their farms
afloat, blowing hard into Tradition's leaky water-
wings before squirming aboard the lifeboat
of B & B Worm Farms, whose salesmen promised
easy money raising worms for agriculture, worms

for industry, worms by the billions, boring
through compost, leaving "castings" to make bumper
crops a cinch—worms that would do all the hard
work, while the farmers could finally buy new
trucks and fly their families to Aruba for some R & R,

never dreaming B & B would be the biggest
pyramid scam in Kentucky history, its owner dying,
leaving the hard-trying farmers' barns stuffed full
of worthless worms—millions of dollars blown
on worms which tried their best to find enough

food in the earth they ate to keep hearts beating,
bodies wriggling once the farmers went bust: compost
and castings abandoned with the worms still struggling
to digest the drying dust that wouldn't feed them,
however hard they tried.

Trouble with The Law

Expect it when you least expect it.
—Overheard

A potato beetle buzzes up the nostril of a drag queen
walking a Shih Tzu. The drag queen grabs her nose
and drops the leash, tripping a bag-hag, whose heart stops.

The Shih Tzu darts into the street, causing a wreck
in which a man loses a leg, a child is paralyzed,
a pregnant witness miscarries twins. The Shih Tzu,

a purebred champion, disappears. The beetle is traced
to Jim's garden, where he negligently used no pesticide.
Soon process-servers mob his door. Several are trampled.

His gate was too narrow; his sidewalk, too hard.
A serial killer/rapist/cannibalistic pedophile is freed
to open up a cell for Jim. His public defender strikes

a deal: Jim pleads guilty to one count of shaving against
the grain, all other charges to be dropped. He agrees,
then learns that, under the New Crime Bill, punishment

for his New Crime is to be hanged, flayed, cut down
while still alive, gutted, drawn, quartered, and burned.
He turns state's evidence against his neighbor who,

without a permit, added a door to his toolshed,
and his other neighbor, who called a white man *niggardly,*
and his other neighbor, who canoed without life vests

for two stowaway thrips. Jim's sentence is reduced
to quadruple amputation, then to one hour on parole
because his cell is needed for a man who wrote a bad

novel with someone else's pen. Lawyers relax
outside the courthouse like Sugar Baby melons, growing
fat and red-ripe in the legal sun.

Where Does Joy Come In?

It sneaks through the cat-flap when you're busy microwaving a beef-
       and-cheese burrito.
It slides down a beanstalk from another galaxy.
It overflows your clogged commode.
It breaks into your triple-locked, burglar-barred life, just before you can
       bolt out the door.

HOW WILL I KNOW IT WHEN IT COMES?

It will be waiting in your bed when you slink home after getting your
       bum drummed, your cashews chewed.
It will be the floating pickerel in a grove of sugar pine.
It will wear a mask identical to its real face.
It will skate up and ask, "Are you a man or a Mouseketeer?"

WHAT WILL IT DO FOR ME?

It will clean your whole house and sleep with you for a veggie burger
       and a mango smoothie.
It will substitute fly-fishing for playing Dudgeons and Drag Queens
       with your friends.
It will stop you for speeding, and write you a ticket to Maui.
It will charcoal on your driveway the phone numbers of lost loves
       whom you should call.

WHAT IF I DON'T WANT IT? WHAT IF IT HURTS TOO MUCH?

Then it will build a body cast around you while you sleep, and pump
       the plaster full of Novocaine.
Then it will bang on your door late at night, screaming, "No fire!"
Then it will take you nude bungee-jumping, stoned out of your tree.
Then it will make an international star of a nobody who looks just
       like you.

HOW DOES IT LEAVE?

It leaves in a taxi between 1 and 4 a.m.
It leaves with a swish of satin, clunk of bowling balls, screech of
caissons, and twitter of bats.
It leaves—between the scent of brimstone and mountain azaleas—
Two scarlet feathers floating in a breeze.

Never Too Late

Doves flute in peeling eucalyptus trees.
      Rain *pit-pit-pit*s off lance-point leaves,
            and pings into expanding bull's-eyes

            on Descanso Pond. Redwings ride
      bucking tules at the water's edge.
Beside them, still as a decoy, a mallard

rests—emerald pate, brass chest,
      pewter sides. Another paddles by,
            leaned forward as if pulled on a string.

            Roses twitch their yellow heads.
      A cottontail pogos away as moss-
backed cooters periscope the pond's scum-crust.

Purple irises bend as if to drink
      when the wind gusts. A school
            of bluegills shadow me. The baking soda

            submarine I lost in 1963
      surfaces: full-sized, blowing
like a whale. The crew flash V for Victory.

The Deed

The same god impels us as impels
The box turtle (red-eyed male—back feet
Trapped by the brown-eyed female's plastron—
Dragged on his back through bracken, over needled
Forest floor), as impels the black
Widow and praying mantis, little males
Sneaking in to pump their seed, even
As the giant females wolf them down.

The very power that drives the male June bug
To mount the female like a two-car pileup,
Commands Great Spangled Fritillaries
To glue their bodies end to end, orange-
And-black wings quivering—the same heat
In their protoplasm as in ours, the need
To replicate, make babies, larvae, fry,
Kits, pups, colts, cubs, young 'uns. The urge

So strong it drives male elk to interlock
Their horns and take two months to die,
Drives humankind to church and lawyers,
Makes them sign papers that bind them
To religious/legal/moral responsibilities,
Makes them create love songs and Wonderbras
And diamond rings, work two jobs, join a health spa,
Gonads pulsing, cells screaming "Divide!"

Ours: the scarlet beat of feathers, the wet press
Of fur, pulse of hind feet that sends sperm shuttling
Toward Ovum, the mother ship. Ours,
The final spurt, last ooze, ultimate
Ahhh—the black-and-yellow exaltation
Of the tiger swallowtail, elation of the crested
Nuthatch, ecstasy of the anopheles,
Sated contentment of the geoduck clam.

Worry Won't Help

The sperm has swum up the right tube,
        or it has not. A fertile egg was there,
or it was not. The sperm did
        or didn't penetrate the egg, which did

or didn't make it without breaking
        down the fallopian waterslide,
and did or didn't implant
        in the uterus, triggering production

of human chorionic gonadotropin,
        which is in her urine, or is not.
Either way, we have options:
        Make love more frequently,

at more fertile times. Play Mozart
        to the fetus in the womb.
The Yes or No aria has been sung;
        now we must dare

to play the tape. Two days
        we've stalled, stuck in the quantum
world where a box can hold a cat
        which is simultaneously dead/

not dead, and stays in that state
        of possibility until the box
is opened, and the cat observed.
        We want to hug our youth tight

and embrace maturity—to stay
        diaper-free, *and* cheer
Little League games which have already
        occurred and not occurred.

That's why my heart stammers,
        and Karen won't get up. She knows
she'll finally fill her plastic cup,
        suck up the product in a dropper,

drip four times into the SAMPLE hole,
        then—as I grip the stopwatch—
wait five minutes while a purple line
        appears, or fails to. Not deciding

the case; stating the verdict.
        One door opens; millions shut.
We are two gods, bringing life
        into this world. Or we are not.

Without a Paddle

He's in a small bay: no big breakers here.
Still, it's scary when his motor stalls.
So much water; so little him. He pulls
the starter-cord hard. Harder. As hard

as he can. He checks the gas gauge.
Pumps more fuel. Adjusts the choke.
Makes sure the motor's out of gear. He hears
other boaters laugh, and understands

that he's a joke: a small man in a small boat,
yanking a cord like some one-armed workout-fiend.
Then, when he decides to row: no oars!
He bobs and dips as bigger boats churn by.

Wakes nearly swamp him. One mistake
and he'll be swimming—which he doesn't, well.
Goddamn engine. Goddamn "Rocky"
at Rocky Point Marina with these goddamn

fucking sad-ass rental boats. His hand
is blistered. His back's giving out.
He's never learned to duel adversity,
and win. Right now, he half-expects his mom

to motor up and save him as he drifts, leaking
outraged dignity. The swells that bounce
his boat make submerged rocks rise
like sea monsters, so he yanks the cord again.

The motor coughs, coughs, dies.
He leans over the side to check the prop.
His glasses slip off his nose into the brine.
He grabs for them; his car keys drop

from his coat pocket. "Shit! Shit! Shit!"
He's close to crying. His windbreaker is soaked.
He yanks the motor cord so hard he falls backward.
The *Crack!* is his new fishing rod. Rocks

chew the bottom of his boat. Oh screw the boat!
Let Rocky sue. Bastard forgot the required
life jacket, too. "This is his damn fault!" he thinks
as the first water sloshes over his new shoes.

Karen, Lost

When, as our line of divers squeezed
        and twisted through the Catalina kelp,
I glanced back and my new wife was gone,
        I gasped as if a Great White
had sliced into me. On every side, green-

        gold fronds shuddered, tall as trees.
Screams die in water, so I bonged my steel
        tank with my knife. Our teacher
finned my way. "Karen's lost!"
        I tried to say in signs, picturing

her eyes as kelp wrapped her, and air
        ran out. My own lungs ached
as Teacher vanished in the fronds,
        then reappeared—in hours,
or instants?—Karen lagging behind.

        As a child, captivated by some squirrel
or toy Santa banging a drum, she drifted
        away from her mom. I waited alone
at the altar, "Here Comes the Bride"
        repeating as she floundered, lost,

through St. Matthew's dark halls.
        Now, belly swollen, breasts too
tender to touch, she's lost again. Will we
        ever find our way back to bass
nibbling from our hands, Garibaldis

        flashing orange, joy lighting twin
bonfires in her eyes? Will she become
        my son's mother, and nothing more?
Will labor drown her, as it has so many
        wives? No use to plead, "Hold

my hand tight." When her mom tied
       a rope to her waist, she slipped
the knot and strolled away. Karen,
       I'll look for you, I swear. I'll bang
on my tank night and day. I'll personally comb

       all Seven Seas, holding in mind your eyes
under the ocean: blissful to be there.
       I'll clasp your hands when you push
through the fronds of childbirth
       and swim with you into the sparkling air.

At Lamaze

"In older times, one in seven mothers died. Today,
it's one in seven hundred," Nurse Laura states with pride.
That means our new friend Lynn, veteran of two
C-sections, would have been a skeleton in older times.

Mary with gestational diabetes, Sam and her breech baby
rot before my eyes. Their husbands mourn,
then remarry, if smallpox doesn't snuff them—
or TB, pneumonia, gangrene from a stinkbug bite.

The whole thing makes me ache to hug every
doctor in sight. Let's throw a party—prime rib,
pastries, open bar—for all pharmaceutical companies.
Go ahead and gouge us. Thank you anyway.

Let's chant a hallelujah chorus to biologists who scour
the Amazon for wonder drugs. Forget global
warming and overpopulation. Forget loss of privacy,
confiscatory taxes, infantilization of the nation

by The Law. Forget my childhood dream of being
Robin Hood. In his twelfth century, I, a breech,
C-section baby, wouldn't have lived to be a father,
wife beside me, son inside her, odds great for us all.

I adore my privileged American life! I adore
my yoga class, executive boxing, electric garage door,
security system with its ululating false alarms.
I adore my insurance agent, my mortgage company,

even the cop who busts me for a bad taillight.
I adore sitcoms I never watch, and newscasts full
of horrors I survived. We'll drive our baby home
to the crib bought by grandparents who, in older times,

would be mold and slime by now. We'll feed vitamins
and Bach to that big brain that makes BIG birth problems,
and may solve them all and more some day.
Spurred by my boy, I'll soon damn bills and taxes louder

than before. I'll swear the country rewards sponging,
and sucker-punches hard workers like me. Still, even
as I declare, "I'm drowning in a sea of lies, pettiness, idiocy,"
I'll know for sure I've won life's lottery.

PART II

Morning Dance

"You never see the same toy turtle twice,"
Heraclitus should have said. My son Erik's chest
of drawers, his Oscar-in-the-Box, his singing
teddy bear: different each time they zing

into his brain, which changes every day.
I'm changing too: Da-Da—a sound attached
at different times to Mom and the TV
by associations he will soon forget, as he'll forget

how, seeing me, he breaks into a dance,
hair spiked from sleep, hands gripping
the top rail of his crib as he shifts weight—
left foot, right foot, left foot, right—

grinning to show eight teeth, and babbling.
Left foot, right, he dances as the weight
of dadhood falls away and I dance toward him:
left foot, right. (I call it *walking*.) Easily

as seven-foot wrestler The Big Show
hurls Stone Cold Steve Austin over the top rope,
I lift my boy over the top bar of his crib
down to the floor. (He'll soon forget

believing I was a Big Show.) I hold
his hands, monkey-style, above his head
as we dance out of the room, me bowlegged
to leave space for him. Left foot, right,

he leads the way as night's curtain lifts,
and day's big band—garbage truck bass,
car-door drums, wren piccolo, cat violin—
bows, and begins.

Cute description of a morning routine and how
the mind remembers objects differently each time
they are thought of.

The Sound That Wakes Me at Night, Thinking of It

Not the victim's wife, sobbing, refusing to get out of bed.
Not his kids, kept home from preschool, snuffling
or wailing, "I want Daddy," when they're not
poking each other or whining, "She hit me!"
Not his brother, jarred awake at 2 a.m., phlegm-
throating, "Fuckers," thinking it took more than one,
fury his finger-in-the-dike that stops a flood.

Not his mother, rocking, wrapped in her own
arms, her face in the bathroom mirror so twisted
and old it stops her cold, the way she might
have stopped him, if *she* hadn't popped pills
to sleep and wake and feel better about her life
that always was, she sees now, fabulously good.
No, it's his father, in court, his speech prepared:

the "impact statement" meant to heap years
of hot-coal suffering on the bastard's head,
since judge and jury—those pukes, those heartless
bleeding ulcers—lacked the stones to squash
a stinkbug. It's Dad, hearing the killer parrot,
"a drug deal gone bad"—that junkie, that syphilitic
gob of tapeworm pus casually adding, as part

of the deal that saved his life, "I popped the kid."
It's Dad, flying over chairs and tables, past
bailiffs and lawyers to reach, somehow,
the killer's throat, his own releasing a sound
between a train grinding to a panic-stop,
and a jet fighter screeching off to bomb Iraq—
sound of a gut-stuck bear before it mauled

Neanderthal—berserker-sound trapped
in suburbia, the one act that could comfort him
choked off by Law, but not the sound
that, even when he's dragged away on national
TV—thrashing, head thrown back, mouth gaped
wide as a bear's—I know he won't stop making,
hour after hour, year after year.

Remembering being in the court room as
  the father is arrested for domestic violence?
  For murder?
—OR—
Remembering being in the court room as anger
  overtakes the father, trying to get at the
  murderer of who?

Sand Fish

It's said they started in beach sand,
but now it's Gobi, Sahara, Mojave grit
the fish sift through their gills, absorbing
oxygen and nutrients while swimming
swiftly as their cousins slide through sea.

They lack all natural enemies—no sand orcas
or seals, sand gulls or pelicans that plunge
into hot dunes to scoop and spear; no sand
fishermen with subterranean hooks and nets;
no sand marlin, sand sharks. The desert

breeds gentle fish. (Abundant sun? Few
clouds? Some quality of superheated air?)
Still, they are rare. The Bedouin who sees one
is called *Allah's Best-Blessed,* and can claim
any camel in the tribe. (This has not happened

in years.) It's said the sand fish have *gone
deep* as tuna do, spooked by a ship. Gone deep,
and learned to slip through rock. I hope
it's true, though it means I'll never see one.
When L.A.'s desert seems hostile to life,

I close my eyes, and sense shapes moving
miles below—megamouth, evolved past
hunger in the stony night; deep-sea anglerfish
with lanterns on their heads that blink like fire-
flies: an intermittent guiding light.

Everything can be okay, if you
adapt to the situation(s).

Duck Tape

> We'll buy three days of food. We'll buy duck tape.
> —Student essay on preparing for terrorist attack

Use Scotch, electrical, or masking, and your ducks
will not hold still. Their wings will flap, their feet
like yellow leaves will kick, their bills will spew
unnerving, stentorian quacks. Who can endure,

when one is stressed, a wiggling duck? We can't
have ducks flopping around if we're attacked.   *Animal*
When poison gases fill the sky, we can't let ducks
plummet from it, crushing our children's innocence.

Nor could we bear, dying of anthrax, to see ducks bob,
blithe as clams—which might be unaffected, too!
We must buy food to last three days, and the right tape
for all our ducks. Why not buy extra rolls, in case

neighbors forget? We must model consideration.
We must keep our spirits up, lining our cupboards,
blocking cracks in our doors with well-taped
mallards, widgeons, pintails, golden-eyes. We'll show

our enemies we're proud, strong, determined not
to die. We'll leave no untaped duck behind.
The only good duck is a taped duck. If it wasn't
for taped ducks, I wouldn't have no ducks at all.

I bless the boy who brings his girl an orange
chrysanthemum plucked from his neighbor's yard,
and a taped duck. I bless the bride and groom exchanging
vows, kisses, and ducks taped mummy-tight.

The farmer's mule may have kicked down the barn
and clopped away, but his ducks stay taped inside.
Beware the duck inadequately taped. Beware its yellow-
topaz eyes.

Making fun of spelling? Duck Tape = Brand
Duct Tape = strong/sticky holding tape
TOTALLY!

I Might as Well Have Begged a Cyclone Not to Spin

I soothed, threatened, cajoled. I returned his howls.
I held him down, stroked his head, commanded
Stop! as my bones quivered in my skin.

Now, having seen how tantrums hurl him
into easeful sleep, I think they're not so different
from what seized me as he was conceived—

seized me, and made me seize my wife's hips ⟩ Sex
and slam into the barrel of her uterus
the charge that would explode into this voice

of ravenous need: the screech of carbon screwing
itself into nitrogen to create life, which, at its heart,
is one long (sometimes pleasurable) scream.

Sex? Talking about Hormone Induced state of Euphoria and dizziness? As cums?

What Kitty Knows

In the same week that John F. Kennedy Jr., with wife
Caroline and her sister Lauren, crashed his private plane
into the sea, a Kentuckian who worked for Tyson Foods—

which gave big money to President Bill Clinton, who led
the mourning for JFK Jr.—fell into, not a vat, *vat* sounds
undignified, like that old song, "I Fell Into a Vat

of Chocolate"; so call it a vast *container,* a *cauldron*
of chicken "parts" being cooked into cat food. And this man—
given three column-inches because death-by-cat-food

struck some editor as cute—this unnamed man was boiled/
drowned/asphyxiated by *9 Lives.* Hey—if half a can
in my cat's dish makes dinner rise in my stomach like the masses

in revolt, what would a whole vast, steaming cauldron do?
Anyway, in the same week John Jr.—"John-John,"
"World's Handsomest Man," as close to royalty as the USA

has got—was gracing more front pages than he did
after his touching-even-if-well-staged salute as the caisson
hauling his dead dad clanged by, Mr. No-Name

(Mr. Hillbilly-Twang? Mr. Loved-A-Sixer-After-Work?),
who maybe thought pro wrestling is real, and Oprah
an intellectual, and watched *America's Vilest Home Videos*

to see the world's fattest (812 pounds) model, the leech-
sucking boy, and the Icelandic girl who made her wedding
dress from frozen spit—this man who may have roared (I did!)

to see that zookeeper's head sucked literally up an elephant's
nether eye, Mr. Zip O. Zilchinsky plunged into Snowball's
breakfast/Mitten's lunch/Fluffy's din-din, died, and had

to share his three inches with No-Name Two, who tried
to save him—a friend maybe, or some Security guy paid
to risk his life like those Secret Service men who failed

to save John-John's dad. In any case, Two tried a rescue
and, "overcome by methane," plunged into the stew
and wasn't laughing, you can bet, when Death's Big Chicken

pecked up his lifeline like a worm. Our country spent millions
to fish out its crashed prince; but I wonder, is it normal
kitty smugness that I see in Matt the Cat's green tiger-eyes,

or some just-ingested knowledge that Man is no Immortal,
and not worthy to drag him from his warm sofa into a cold night
comfortless as the bottom of the sea?

The Last Bobcat

The hill behind our house still wears its cape
of African daisies. The poison oak hummock
still thrusts out stinging green where he crouched:
brown menace that made me think *coyote*.

But the ears he thrust up were tufted, turning
to cup sound. His eyes sparked green.
We stared at each other, balanced
between predator and prey. He could have been

a lion, poised to grow full-sized in a few
bounds. I shrank indoors, heart galloping.
He stepped from cover then: black-tipped ears;
twitching white bob-tail; tomcat face slashed

with black war-paint; muttonchop sideburns
swept out, downcurving to a stubbled chin.
The hill absorbed him as his paws absorbed
the sound of their own passing. The black

splotches on his flanks turned back to rock;
the tawny hide merged with brown earth.
Now every time I step outside, I look for him
crouched on the roof to spring, or frozen, mid-

stalk, in the yard. His absence pads down
the deer trail. His dearth shadows the poison oak.
His lack can rise out of the hill at any time.
Each splash of light could be his unforgiving eye.

Don' Like

The Arabs who invented Algebra can't have known
Miss Seitz would teach it, any more than Einstein
knew he'd be the Father of Catastrophe.

The Miss which prefaced her name proudly
(would no man have her, or would she have no man?)
made me think Mistake, Mischance, Miserable

Misfit, Missing Link, Lord of Misrule.
Only the fiends who stoked the furnace of eighth grade
were glad to see her hunched at her desk, gutting

papers with her bloody pen. X's identity counted
for nothing, next to perfect headings: student's name,
class name and period, *her* name, and the date

in that order, starting exactly three lines from the top,
margins one inch, paper creased in perfect thirds
(no crooked ends, no refolding), or she would fix you

in a basilisk stare, shove back your work, and hoarse
as a reanimated corpse, croak, *Don' Like.*
What math we gained is gone now as Del Shannon's

"Runaway"—as Billy Tilly's spit-shined shoes,
and the blade Ray Montez applied to my throat, hissing,
"Gimme all your cash, you little fruit"—gone

as the mush-burgers Ms. Hairnet slapped down
on our lunchroom trays—as Teddy Jones,
falling between the granite blocks at Freeport Jetty,

crawling back up, extending the cracked glass stump
of his new Pfleuger rod, groaning, *Don' like.*
The words remain: an anthem as I near Miss Seitz's age.

Hip-hop and bottles crashing next door after 9:00—
the candidates and their campaigns—
the way my clothes fit, and the barber cuts my "hair"—

hot salad and cold soup served by a pretty waitress
who thinks middle-aged manhood's a dirty joke—
Time's scaly hand, Xing, in red, my dwindling . . .

I think everyone has had at least one teacher

like this, if not, they are very lucky souls.

Summer of Love

The blue lilies have turned to powder where you stood
shaking sun-sequins from your hair. The same
palm trees host different bat-ears and crab-eyes.

It felt so good to melt in sea, to meld with sky,
I wish I'd had a silver net to catch that day.
I wish I'd had hot bronze to dip it in,

so I could touch it on my mantel any time.
Just wisps remain: pale blurs of skin,
an empty beach, a purple blanket in the shade

of my red VW van, sun flaming off Galveston sand
as your green bikini wiggled to your feet,
and the war in Vietnam lurched, bleeding, by.

I'll pretend we blasted Hendrix's "Little Wing."
I'll pretend we fired a bowl of Kona gold.
I'll pretend we're still in one another's arms,

our cries like the gulls' that soar and glide
and rise high in the humid air where we still float
under this Texas sun, somewhere.

Nerves of Titanium

Handcuffed and chained,
he uses a concealed
lock-pick to escape
a coffin buried in hot
sand. The chain-
wrapped cage dropped
into Arctic water
through a hole drilled
in three feet of solid ice
can't hold him. But
what yanks me upright
in my motel bed
is when—double-
cuffed, straitjacketed—
he's shoved out
of an airplane. If he
can't pull his parachute
cord in ninety seconds,
he won't need
to find a new career.

I, who get dizzy
on a curb, watch
his thin hands
probe and pluck
while skydivers film
his every twitch. I,
who absorbed calculus
with Hendrix twanging
and my roommate
banging his girl behind
a glass-bead door,
have attention deficit
disorder compared to
this freak: lock-picking
while he falls twice

as fast as if he took
the standard limbs-
spread starfish pose.
What if he breaks
his tiny pick? Or
drops it? What
if his hands shake,
or get too cold
to work a lock? (Mine
do, just watching.)

Keats, bent over
his odes; Newton,
his calculus;
Beethoven, his Ninth—
Tiger on the green,
Kobe at the line,
Rice snagging a pass
while tacklers
howitzer at his head—
all were hysterics
next to this nut
from Tennessee.
"He never hung out
much with girls.
He'd ruther play
with his handcuffs,"
his mother drawls.

"Wish he had his old
job back at Burger King,"
sighs his wife
as he begins to spin.
He's toast, I think—just
as he lifts his hands,
his orange chute

blossoms overhead,
and—see!—he comes
floating, God-like,
down to crowds
who praise him
from the ground,
or (ignoring spousal
snores, as well as sex-
squeals from next
door) cheer,
from motel beds
across this land, a man
apart. Unlike us.
Lock-pick in hand.
Free.

Houdini? From wife's perspective?

Liar's Ball

My wife points to pencil-snarls scrawled on the wall.
"Erik, who did this?" "Da-Da!" he pipes cheerfully.
Wham-bam, he's in a chandeliered ballroom with Peter,

who denied Christ; Clinton, who disclaimed Paula;
Arnold Upchurch, who disputes DNA, wailing,
"I didn't do it," as the state's poison pours in. Hurray—

we're at the Liar's Ball, where Erik, tuxed by Baby
Gap, is Toddler King. We wear false faces, and dance
the Duplicity here. We play Prevaricator's Waltz

in shifting keys. "Da-Da!" Erik cries to wild applause,
hands raised like goalposts, fibbing's football tumbling
through. My squawk-puppet's a real boy now.

He's joined the League of Lying Animals—totem,
the angler fish; mascot, the trap-door spider. He wears
the sacred T-shirt: Adam, whining, "What apple?!"

"The bosses can hijack your body any time," I tell him.
"But your mind's a temple. Never tell them how you dance
in there."

Nuh-Nuh-Nuh-Nuh-Nuh-Nuh-Nuh-Nuh-Nuh, *Dah* Dah Dah! Doesn't Look Like Much in Print

Hammered, though, on Led Zeppelin's bass and guitar,
didn't those sounds surge and shake like Linda in Mom's
Simca with the stuffing coming out? Weren't they my fists,
making a strawberry frappé out of Fred's mouth

(the double-crossing sack of scat)? Didn't they catch
the shimmering green-gold of dorado flipping,
flopping, flying, trying not to die after they slammed
my Deceiver, then ripped up the Sea of Cortez while Jesus,

my guide, coached me in speed-metal Spanglish?
Seguro que by God *si!* The shoe-sized, scrambling roach
that made Cecilia scream, the urinal ice that shrinks
in your hot stream—it's all in those staccato chords.

But does *staccato* say it? Sorry, not today.
Can words compete with "Meditation" from *Thais*?
No alliteratin' way. It's the best kiss you ever had,
the most beautiful bed-partner: squish of lips and brush

of thighs, mountain bluebirds in the trees, and butterflies—
painted ladies, red admirals, spicebush swallowtails,
but mourning cloaks too, because the kiss subsides,
the ladies die, ants gang-drag them away. Under

the beauty, there's that coyote's-caught-a-housecat squeal
that jerked you out onto your porch, dark churning in.
"Does Your Chewing Gum Lose Its Flavor on the Bedpost
Overnight?" isn't poetry, but when the banjo bangs

as Lonnie Donegan noses the tune—hey, it's leaping out
of bed for summer swimming and cartoons. It's thrash-
in-the-grass hilarious when you and friends are wasted,
whacked-out, fecal-faced. It's vaulting off your pew,

high-stepping down the aisles, cold-cocking deacons
with collection plates. What good are whiff-of-pancake
words when you crave a steaming stack; a glimpse
of thigh, when you're starved for the whole girl? Forget

the IRS and idiot President; "Stars and Stripes Forever"
flaps me like a flag. I dump irony out of my duffel bag,
and cry to think how many died in World War II
so Santa could bring me a hi-fi to play "Rave On"

and "Topsy II," every blood cell banging its bongo
with Cozy Cole, every neuron igniting when Buddy sang,
"Uh weh heh heh heh hell . . ." No way in heh heh hell
can words say that, or tell how good it felt to jam

my sunburst Stratocaster in my crotch and hump like Hendrix
whanging "Little Miss Lover," wah-wah pedal plugged
into my spine, sound roaring out the way the world
roared out of God—plum trees, ferrets, the Appalachians

and Ganges, crabgrass and brown recluse spiders, Ford
Falcons and dudes named Buck and Fabian, chicks
named Tiffany and Krys, and winning the Big Fish Pool
on the Lindy Lou with a lingcod longer than I was tall at ten,

and no-handing my bike home from Natalie's after we kissed—
A WHUNK da ta WA ta, a WHUNKa whunk WHAA
flash-flooding out of me: rock-Yahweh with a guitar I loved
so much that, when some crackhead robs my home,

it isn't my computer full of poems I mourn, but that guitar—
the notes it still had left to play—the night when, bound
for a real job with a real salary, I tucked my love into its case,
and lugged the case, black as a coffin, off the stage.

Sad for the Hunchback

This sounds bad already, I know; but
when I saw her buying cheese in Trader Joe's—
four-foot-ten, a gourd-like hump lumping

under her green blouse—my stomach
flinched as if I'd just been clubbed. I wanted
to cry, "Unnh," picturing mountains

of rejection behind her. (I didn't mean that play
on words, but leave it. I'll bare my technique.)
I know the truth, her meek face roared.

Rumpelstiltskin could spin a sweater
from my pale chin-hair. No use having it
removed. I'm a hunchback. Who'd care?

I stood there, dying to express my "Unnh"—
not to show off my compassion's tall, handsome
muscularity, I swear—because I felt so sad

for her: *Passed over. Left out. Oh, unfair . . .*
Of course I know how patronizing
this will seem. You have to *be* a hunchback

to write about one—or dead like Victor H
and Dylan T—and *great,* artistically and ethically—
the polar opposite of me, who jerked big

laughs, one June night, out of Miss Spokane,
declaring, *Ugly people shouldn't have genitals*
because IT MAKES ME SICK. So what

if I nearly cried to read about a man with an IQ
of 50, kicked to death in a "locked facility"?
So what if, at Oak Forest Elementary, back

in the Pleistocene, I gave a Valentine to Joe
Touchton with his withered arm, and Charlie Croch—
scorned for his name, his inability to throw

or catch a ball—*and* who, in high school,
turned out to be gay? Who won't believe I love
to praise myself, and this is one more way?

Equal Rights, Rights for the disabled, LGBTQ Rights, etc.

One Week Until Opening Day

"Shiver! Shiver! Shirt, shirt, shirt!" the mockingbird
shrills as I lift my fishing flannels from their drawer.
"River! River! Beef jerky, jerky, jerky!" the bird cheers

as I fondle my fingerless wool gloves and can of wader-
patching goo. I revel in my reels, my spools of line: fifteen-
pound-test, six-pound-test, weight-forward, bass taper,

sink tip. I gloat like Scrooge McDuck to see the glittering
lures that overflow my tackle box: Hula Popper, Jitterbug,
Rattletrap, crank baits, buzz baits, spinner baits, plus

snarls of hooks, jigs, plastic worms, Daredevil spoons
fiery with wiggle and flash. All hail Alligator Sunscreen,
that scares skin cancer's man-eating crabs away!

I'm wild to gallop through spring mud beside a stream—
to shiver in dawn chill, numb fingers pumping my float tube—
to load my rods onto a boat as buddies razz, "Uh-oh,

look who cleaned out the store." A puff of down, long-
grounded, leaps into the air as I lift my fly-tying gear.
How can I overstate my feelings for the rooster saddle, gaudy

as an Aztec priest; the vise, collapsed and shimmering;
the thread and bobbin, hair-stackers and dubbing-twisters?
Soon I'll be whip-finishing flies. Soon they'll skip over

slippery riffles, skate through slicks, bip-bap-bop
along rocky bottom where the lunkers lie. I bless my vest
heavy with forceps, split shot, clippers, leaders, floats,

my flies lined up in schoolboy rows: Adams, Cahill,
Quill Gordon, Blue Dun, and his brother, Pale Morning.
It's sad they stab the mouth of Cousin Trout; but man,

their names feel good in mine. I praise my own fumbling
hands that tied this Skykomish Sunrise, this Beatis Parachute.
I praise my lost friend Jon, who taught me the roll cast.

I praise my dad, who bought my first fishing rod,
and drove me to a muddy pond where I cranked in a jeweled
bluegill, and Mom pan-fried it for two bites of bony meat.

"Chillywilly, chill! chill!" calls the mockingbird. "Sweet-
heart, sweet-heart!" And my heart trills, "See, see, see, see!
Delight! Delight!"

"Man Stuck in Spiderweb,"

Erik announces, the morning after Sea World.
"Man stuck in spiderweb," he states,
slurping milk with Frosted Flakes. "Man

stuck in spiderweb," he warns Grandma
by phone. Not a word about squeak-talking
dolphins or the plumber-seals who unclogged

whale-sized toilets for their walrus-boss.
What he remembers is the 3D movie-pirate,
all *avast*s and unconjugated *be*s, stumbling

through Dead Man's Cave into a web
big as a medieval tapestry, home to a spider
with red tennis shoes and soulful eyes.

Erik knows how it feels to be stuck
in a bath or on a doctor's table—trapped
no matter how he kicks and cries.

He may not grasp the subtleties of death
or time, but he feels their sticky strands;
he understands the metaphor that normally,

in this land of optimists, hides in the dark,
but comes now to his call, on unshod feet,
crawling.

PART III

Manpanzee,

they called him: throwback to saber-tooths and caves.
Jim, his handler, kept his body shaved, and raised him
like a monkey-Mozart: prodigy who understood
English, could dress himself, and count to twenty

on fingers and toes. He thought he was human, poor
ugly duck, and cried to be more like the smooth-skinned
boys who spoke so well, and kept his ape-lips shut.
But when the circus closed, Jim had to hawk used cars

and marry a widow with two human sons. Barred
from the house, Manpanzee was sold. A zoo. An end
to shaves, shirts, pants, and shoes—to Frosted Flakes
with milk, and tetherball. No need to practice hand signs

no one understood. Back with the slow kids, Manpanzee
was forced to grab, with hands that had lifted
China teacups, the browning "greens," moldy apples,
and bananas dumped on his "habitat" floor.

Ten years dragged by like one interminable humping
by the hairy, hooting trolls inside his cage—and out.
Then one day the keepers, armed with poisoned darts
in case he went ape, led him to a room where TV

cameras burned. *He likely won't know you,* a chesty
redhead warned a sweating man. But even bloated
and gray, the man was Jim: blue eyes brim-full
of feeling with no place to go. If Manpanzee could

have whispered, *Daddy, it'll be all right,* he would have
as his long arms hugged that thin, quivering back.
But only ape-noises squeezed out—
and what the snickering newsman called *monkey-tears.*

ARCHITECTURE

It Had to Do with Candy Sanders:

How I went coat-less to show her I was brave.
How, when we danced the schottische in P.E.,
my breathing shook. How I strained to see
her panties when she whirled. It was fun

to ride my bike, repeating *Can-dy,* one syllable
per pump. But Little Anthony sobbing,
"Tears on My Pillow," Ben E. King's cavernous,
"I—I who have no one . . ." warned of worse

pain to come than broken arms and stitches—
adult pain like heart attack, or what pinned
Mr. Jones in bed all day: a grown man, crying.
I had Teddy Laughlin to catch bluegills with,

Joey Franz for Home Run Derby, Zack
and Jack Boles to toilet-paper houses. I had
my sister Carol to tease, her cats to torment,
and my mom and dad. Could it all be raygun-

blasted into nothing by a girl when I rowed
past the known world out onto the pitching
whitecaps of my teens? When Candy traded
dog tags with Trenton Glass, I hummed, "Tragedy,"

but still stayed on my toes at shortstop,
snagged the ball's white blur, and threw a strike
to Robbie Tate at first. He'd turn gangster,
and OD at seventeen; but at ten he yelled,

"Way to rock, Doc," as I jogged in to bat,
loose and easy as the yodel on "Little Star,"
the singer begging for "a love to share." How
would it be to want someone so much I cried?

To live in Lonesome Town or Heartbreak Hotel?
To hurt like Jack Scott, voice smoky and deep
as he moaned, "Burning bridges behind me,"
and the pines in my backyard shuddered and sighed?

We Could've Been Commandos,

creeping through dark woods toward the parked Ford,
        then hunkering behind a pine to light
our firecracker-strings. Juan leaped high
        onto the Ford's hood, stomped quick flamenco,
and dropped his "grenades." Frank and I
        lobbed ours, which volleyed as we ran.

Behind us, the Ford's headlights flamed. A man
        bailed out, pants to his knees. "Assholes!" he screamed.
While his girl (naked, we knew) cringed on the floor,
        we leapt into his high beams, bared our butts
and, hooting, hightailed it through a blackberry maze.
        Mission accomplished, we believed—until orange

gunfire cracked the dark. Bullets whanged overhead,
        clipping leaves, seeking flesh to bury in.
"Oh shit, oh fuck," we moaned: dead boys, running.
        Miles from the road, panting, we stopped, and lit
what Juan jabbed at us. "Jeez, the asswipe tried to kill us . . ."
        Triumph settled in: we'd come through

our first firefight! "She had big white titties,"
        Juan crowed. "And a red beaver, I swear."
"You never saw that," I declared as three bones grew.
        Frank punched his radio. A whiny mouth-organ
tuned in, then two-part harmony—*Love, love me do*—
        a bullfrog and a spring peeper, bobbing to a beat

too slow for fast, too fast for slow. "The rock sensation
        that's sweepin' the nation," some deejay blared.
"Sensationally lame," I said. "Tea-sippin' fairies,"
        Juan sneered as cicadas gusted through the trees.
Across the sea, girls surged at the Beatles in waves.
        It was June: two months before school's mangle

started up again. We might have all done "it" by then.
        Some nympho with big titties and a red beaver
might pick us up, and teach us everything.
        Our futures—so nearly shot down—rose up alive
and solid from the forest floor: the Bouncing
        Betty that would take Juan's leg; the blast

of faith that knocked Frank out of college
        onto Portland's streets, where he pogoed in orange
Hare Krishna robes, then married
        a woman with three kids, and disappeared;
the twenty-buck guitar that, strumming "Love
        Me Do" on stage at Pagoda a Go Go,

exploded my anonymity, and blew me up
        out of my tract home in Houston, Texas,
where my parents watched *I Dream of Jeannie,*
        sure I'd be a brain surgeon and buy the house
next door—blew me up, lifted and spun me,
        with my boots and Super Beatle amp,

through rolling doobies for the Byrds,
        scoring coke for Cream, shooting junk
with strippers at The Booby Hatch—lifted and spun me,
        then dropped me, strung out, in the muck.
I've crawled for years through hostile lines, carrying
        this dispatch. Here.

GREAT IMAGERY WITH SOLID STORY.

Lingerie Show STRIPCLUB?

She does the hip-cocked, hands-behind-head, I-just-happen-
to-be-standing-here-in-pink-thong-panties grin. She does
the hand-on-thigh, you-know-I'm-braless-under-my-blue-
teddy, *Hello there*. She does the baby-doll-in-see-
through-nightie, stunned by the soft slap of her own sexiness.

We guys are doing I'm-just-here-with-my-pot-gut-bad-tie-
weak-drink-and-half-a-stiffie, or Don't-know-how-I-got-here-
but-I've-seen-better, or I-came-in-for-a-Scotch-and-saw-
this-chick-so-fut-the-whuck-I-stayed. I think she loves being
the one bunny in a pen with mangy coyotes, three-legged

bobcats, crush-backed snakes. She's still a virgin here,
smashed on estrogen, sky-high on her new curves, no idea
what men think of flesh they pay to see. She could be
a coed cutting Comp, a receptionist with "glamour" photos
in her Hyundai's trunk, or Daddy's girl, wiggling free

from his estate with guesthouse and Olympic pool.
Behind a model's makeup and insouciance, her smile
pleads, *Love me;* so the world will break her heart.
Maybe I'll pass her in Safeway one day—hair hacked off,
waist thick, three kids screeching for Captain Crunch,

not Cheerios. *Penthouse* could call to offer a side slot
(so few issues, so many girls): five hundred bucks
for some pink shots. Maybe I'll see her on TV, or offering
out-call massage in some weekly throwaway. She could
get a PhD, and lock away the photos Goatee Geezer's

taking now: proof what a prize she used to be.
"See," she'll tell her husband, "I was almost beautiful"—
this shining girl caught in the world's high beams;
Fame, in his black limo, whispering, "Baby, every road
leads up from here."

COMICAL

The Best Moment of My Life

[handwritten: NOT CAPITALIZED... WHY?]

may have been five minutes ago, warm air shurring
through vents above the bed, wife crunching Corn Flakes

in the kitchen, son asleep, an ache in my left ankle
adding just a twinge to foreground the perfection.

Or maybe it's now, as I press arms above my head—
stretch, groan, then do a slow motion frog-kick

under my white, smooth-as-shave-cream sheets.
It could have been the time I leaned back in my swing,

and the sky became green grass spears,
while a sky-blue earth took shape under my feet—

or when—Julie on her balcony—I played Romeo
until an orange fireplug tackled me, making her laugh,

then mouth, "I love you" as I sprawled on my back,
and the night, except for one cricket, went still.

But what can beat right now: bare feet on cool floor
as I pull the blinds, and they squeak open on my son's

red dolphin swing, green froth of shrubbery,
one yellow rose behind the perfumed ear of spring?

[handwritten: NOT OVERLY FLOURISHED - MORE REAL]

[handwritten: USE OF I ALLOWING READER TO BE A PART CREATING A MORE INTIMATE POINT OF VIEW AND EXPERIENCE.]

[handwritten: ENJOYING THE SIMPLE THINGS, FOCUS ON THE BODY AND WHAT IS GOING ON AROUND THE NARRATOR.]

Word of Mouth

for Andranik Shakhbazyan

Five minutes after my wife leaves for an oil change
at Andy's Texaco three blocks away,
she's back to tell me, "Andy died." Pewter-haired

Andy, who called customers "my friend"
in his accent smooth as hummus, rich as *mutabal,*
who changed my oil, fixed my clutch,

and when my brakes went out before a job interview,
dropped everything to get me on the road.
Andy, who'd fill any kid's bike tires for free,

who said with pride, "My business is all word-of-mouth,"
who never overcharged, did work I didn't need,
or failed to have my car ready on time.

Heaped banks of flowers—roses, mums,
carnations; yellow, pink, white, peach, indigo—
guard the station's door when I drive by.

In my garden, a light breeze wags the burst
stamens of green corn. The sun's yolk strains   LEAD HERE THROUGH
to squeeze through the gray, curdled sky.   THE ORDINARY.

One day someone will say to someone else
who barely knew me, but I hope liked me
as much as I liked Andy, "Charlie died."

IMPACT OF BEING "HONEST"

Marco Polo

The swimmers who halloo his name
honor the Khan's Venetian friend, I assume,
as I belt my son into his Safe T. Seal life vest.

It's good that these kids haven't heard
the great Marco was a great fraud
who never made it east of Baghdad . . .

"Marco!" shouts a red-goateed boy
as I tow my son across the pool.
"Polo!" the boy's friends roar, and dodge

his gropes and lunges while, yards
away, the ocean's glittering blue
heaves and humps toward Xanadu.

Diving at dawn with parrot fish and yellow
tangs, I felt part of the sea's great
fellowship. Now—oldest in the pool—

I'm more apart than *It,* who foghorns,
"Marco," homing in on a pink
micro-suit, a khan's ransom of flesh

he's privileged to clutch wherever
his hands run aground. How can he know
his course leads straight to me?

"Daddy!" my son shrills, "Shark attack!"
Great white adult, I chomp
my snorkel, slide my mask into place,

and as I make my shark-descent,
allow myself one glimpse of teenaged skin
from my own past that grows more

distant as I sink, and some lost kid calls—
above the water or below?— "Marco!
Marco . . ."

Bimbo Limbo

> Your old girlfriends are all in Bimbo Limbo.
> —Overheard

But wait! The loves who pumped my life's balloon
when it threatened to drop me into jungles of ebola,
seas of krakens, fast-lanes full of 18-wheelers with lung-

shriveling breath—they can't have shuffled off . . .
Oh, maybe one or two—breast cancer, car wreck, some disease
I've never heard of, nor had she when Doc mumbled,

"I have bad news." The others are (I pray) like me,
still keeping heads out of the river, enjoying the swim
and view, though the current's picking up, the roar ahead

undeniable now as mist-clouds from the shark-
toothed rocks on which the water, after a mile's lacy
dawdle-dive, explodes. Still, limbo wouldn't be so bad.

Plato's there—and Aristotle, Socrates, Pythagoras,
Euripides . . . think of the brainy conversations!
And don't think my former flames couldn't join in.

Didn't they have the great good sense to fall for me?
I'm only kidding. No I'm not. Yes I am; I don't believe
in limbo any more than hell or paradise not of this earth.

Seeing the young Britney's heavenly thighs and below-
the pubis jeans, though—and Pam before her chest apotheosis-
sized—and Jessica, who *can* sing, and didn't really say,

"The capital of Hawaii is H," and, let's face it, looks
fantastic in cutoffs . . . watching that trio do the Bimbo
Limbo—*How low can you go?*—sounds good to me.

A place where that happens can't be too far
from heaven, especially if my old girlfriends are there,
God being Beauty, after all, God being Love.

Catfish

In tight, bright shorts and halter tops, the girls
look good enough to eat. The flashy red-yellow-

     and-blue ball they're bopping back and forth
     looks better still, to the cruising flathead cat.

When the ball plops in the lake, the flathead
strikes, jamming the ball tight in its craw.

     No matter how the big fish fights, it's buoyed up.
     No matter how onlookers hoot, how hard

they hurl their sticks and stones, the giant
can't dive to its hide-hole in the muck.

     Picnickers slosh to the attack in boats and tubes.
     Life is pain. Give it, and get used to it,

they sneer, like Romans praising the old ways.
God Himself drops down from a Peterbilt truck

     to poke the fish with a ski-pole, gleeful
     as when He tortured Job like a stinkbug.

Then a pale man in a straw hat flops onto a tube
and thrashes toward the fish. It has stopped

     circling, and floats: gills blood-red, quivering.
     God sees the pale man's pocketknife,

and sneers, "Stick'im." The pale man lifts his blade.
Dodging slime-slick fins that could spindle

     his hand and sink his tube, he stabs.
     The ball shrinks with a hiss. The pale man—

frightened, all his life, of fish—still slides his hand
into the whiskered mouth, and plucks out the ball.

      The flathead dives. God and the beach crowd
      sigh and turn away, taking no notice

when the pale man parts a flap in the June air
and slips through, back to his alien land.

Day Before Memorial Day

Let the usual mockingbirds, like gold-chained rappers
perched on your satellite dish, holler down their boasts and jeers.
Let sun slide toward your window one inch at a time,

a rising light-tide that lifts you toward another forgettable
day. No need yet for gentlemen to start their engines.
Tomorrow will be time to see how fast people can drive

to honor those who died with bowels bayoneted,
limbs blown off, skulls pulverized, or more slowly
of typhus, gangrene, septicemia so that you, snoozing

in your king-sized bed, can feel martyred when your cat
plucks the door-screen, yowling to come in. As you rolled
grounders to your son last night, that cat pranced by,

a squealing rat dangling like a Fu Manchu. She dropped it
behind the hedge to torture more, the way you tossed
still-hooked bluegills back into White Oak Bayou to force out

more fight. As you scrape rat guts off your porch,
try not to think of wars your ancestors survived, passing
their murderous DNA to you, which must be why you ache

to gun your way through traffic jams, and garrote *authorities*
who set serial killers free, but won't let you shoot BBs
in your own backyard. It must be why, watching

The Last Samurai, your five-year-old grabs his plastic sword,
hacks the air, and screams so loud your wife threatens
to slap him if he doesn't "simmer down," and let her enjoy

the on-screen butchery. While terrorists build atom bombs,
and Operation Break-a-Camel's-Back drags on and on,
you can relax with the sports page full of projectiles and clubs,

hits and *kills* and *sudden death.* It's all in fun. Have some,
for the love of Christ (who also died for you, and not
comfortably). Save for tomorrow your reflections

on the custard-brains who think they can scold Hitlers
out of their *Dachau*s. Give up your shame at having killed
no enemies. You can slip by Memorial Day the way

you snuck past Vietnam. (What joy to hear, "unfit to serve."
For once, the government was right!) You'll swim today
at your father-in-law's club, its yearly dues more than your father's

salary. Savor the pool's tanzanite blue. Plunge into familial
love, and come up sputtering. Sip Irish Cream after coaching
your son's tee-ball team to a rare victory. Toss pinecone

grenades at a yapping wiener dog. Count yourself blessed
that your country holds a place called *Dickeyville Grotto,*
and any time you like, you can go there.

Brain Silos

If weirdness is beauty, and beauty, truth, weirdness is true.
—Marginalia

Does each silo plunked down along this highway
hold the living brains of movie stars or geniuses
contemplating gravity, the spotlight, perfect
sentences, the thrill of atoms trilling in platinum-
bombshell hair? Or are they average brains,

shucked from the heads of plasterers and managers
of donut stores—cab driver, shoe salesman,
swimming teacher brains, rejoicing not to be
pinches of slush, flakes of jerky, or lumps
of nothing, like the flesh they used to ride?

Are my spirits high because my brain's so close
to its own kind, thinking of dance lessons and peach
cobbler, fixing screen doors and de-fleaing cats—
average thoughts like those that floated
up from Candlelight Lane on August evenings,

bobwhites whistling, Mom frying chicken, Dad
just home from work, tackled by kids before he plopped
into his Big Chair—thoughts of bluegill fishing
and hot grounders, swing sets and cheerleader
tryouts—no red envelopes marked "Final Warning,"

no coke-addict daughters or catastrophic
mammograms—generous thoughts, well able
to embrace a field of wheat under a sky heaped high
with clouds—happy thoughts, filling the air
parting in front of us like herds of Jersey cows

clogging the road—thoughts that cushion me,
my wife, and our son, who heard *brain*

when I said *grain*, from the world's jolts and jarrings
as I laugh, and yell "Good thinking!" to the silos
as our Rent-a-Wreck blasts by.

Blue lupines and pink Nootka roses tint
    the borders of this silver
        tentacle that twists and glitters
            twelve hundred miles from my home.

        Cottonwood lint fills the air.
      In the current, rocks make breakers-in-reverse,
    as if this creek runs backward, or the rocks
are mottled manatees struggling upstream

as root-snarls whack against the bank
    and tree limbs coil like razor wire
        in the prison flick I saw last night.
          The killer's girl could've been Tess

        Perry's twin: same nose a little bit too
      thin, same oval face, same peach-
    slice lower lip, same upward-glancing, wide-set
eyes that dunked me in the icy shock of love.

Tess-at-eighteen seemed reborn, just as Widow's Creek,
    Oregon, or Crab Creek, Maine, are reborn here.
      I breathe the scent of snowmelt spiced
        with algae the same way, lips on her neck,

      I breathed the scent of Tessi's hair.
    White noise surrounds me, rising
  from the froth like radio static
drowning girl-voices I almost understand . . .

No wonder Greeks believed in water nymphs.
    No wonder I called Tessi in the shower *my naiad*.
    All cultures link women with water.
      Everywhere the human thought-stream

            carves the same spirals and curves.
         On Castle Creek, robins and magpies squeak
     from shadows that crouch low, defying light.
Three feet from me, a branch of overhanging

spruce trails in the flow. My son—born
     to a woman unlike Tessi on the surface,
         but under it the same water-
              sacked-in-skin—this boy I love more

             than myself (he *is* my younger, stronger self)
        trails his fingers while our boat slices
     Gull Lake—his small hand skittering
like a coot, wobbling like a steelhead spoon,

scudding like a catamaran, the way my own hand did,
      trailing out my dad's truck window,
         bounced by currents of this same warm air
          that floods back every spring.

Handling a Trophy Trout

When she's too tired to reach the mossy rocks
where, slurping blue-winged olives, she took mine,
I lift her head out of the water, kneel,
and, rod-tip high to mute the thrashing, slide her
across the varnished table of the stream.

Behind, layers of sediment lift into cliffs—
rust-brown, aqua-blue, dry-grass-green:
a stack of pages millions of years old,
sawed through one by one, grain after grain,
by the ice water into which I plunge

my hand, and with numb fingers, pinch the fly.
It's stuck, so I grip the slippery-smooth fish-
flesh, and flip her. Belly up, she lies still
as if hypnotized. Above the canyon walls,
a river of blue sky eddies with clouds.

Cat-paws of wind smack the real river
into chop. Admiring the olive body peppered
with black dots, the crimson stripe down
silver sides, I free the hook, then, as the river
laps my knees, slide the fish in.

She doesn't swim, so I move her back
and forth, forcing water through her gills.
Downstream, where Bighorn Canyon Road
crawls from the river, I see faces
in the rock: owls, demons, Indian gods.

How many generations stand behind me!
How many deaths my ancestors, human
and not, endured to pass life on to me!
I feel it rise in the fish as she slips free
from my hand, picking up speed, gliding

over algaed rock toward where the current calls.
I watch her melt into the river: her home,
as the air is mine that fills my lungs
and stings my eyes as I stand, dripping:
re-baptized: reborn.

Dismantled for Goodwill, Our Son's Crib

leans against our bed. The ship-of-slats that ferried him
through his first years, traps us in its floating cage
as my wife and I slip down sleep's muddy stream.

That crib spent hard time in the Don't Wear closet
with outmoded pants, shirts, dresses, shoes,
while we postponed our second child.

When my wife passed her fertile crescent, entering
the dry scrublands, we kept the crib
for *sentimental reasons*, like a teddy bear in a flash flood.

Change *fear*'s *ea* to *ou*, and we could have *four* kids,
the crib's white gloss four times more
scratched, scraped, chewed, the house swollen

with four times the cacophony, four times the chaos,
four chances for an Einstein, Shakespeare,
Mozart, Ruth, but also a Goebels, a Night Stalker,

a bag-man chattering to Martians as he shoves
his shopping cart along—four chances to buy
a small coffin to fill a little grave—four creditors

hammering at our door, garnishing our energy
and self-centeredness, which is why we waited
too long, and the Magic Kingdom closed.

But let's not talk about that. Let's talk about the crib
rebuilt inside another house, a new father
fitting the pieces as I did the day after my son was born.

"The tide has turned," a voice whispered in my head.
"The wind is right as it will ever be. The ship waits.
Bring your new life home."

Corn

I'm slurping lemon yogurt when sound surges
from my radio like liquid diamonds, or sunlight
mixed with honey and titanium—so sweet and ringing,
delicate yet strong-as-continental-drift, I can't
describe it without sounding corny and wanting to cry.

It glides inside me, soft as the vapor-hands of a girl
who died. She loved her hamster, Lemon Jello,
and watched him gallop in his yellow wheel for hours.
Her parents wanted everything for her, but then one day
a garbage truck . . . Oh stop! My composure's

tottering after this week's-worth of bunker-buster bombs.
And now this sound—all right, this *voice*—human,
I guess—this woman, singing—shifts blocks inside
my chest, yanks pulleys, twirls knobs, spins gears,
cranks levers gently as Mom's (sorry!) purple pansies

swaying in a warm dawn breeze. I'm groping—"Eight-
letter vulgarism for *dysfunctional*?"—when the singer—
barely 5'3', with curled, platinum hair—materializes
by the fridge, her every atom pulsing supernova,
black hole, $E = mc^2$ energy. All I want is to solve

my crossword, forget work, maybe share a wine
cooler with my wife—no fights, no loathsome discussions—
as my son adds fractions without a fuss. Wanting
too much keelhauls the soul. Mine can't endure more
flaying barnacles, shark-chompings, brine instead of air.

Sure, it was great to scuba dive with green turtles
and yellow tangs, young myself, my wife so sexy
in her mask and fins, our every touch was making love.
But now, when adult life roars, *Atten-HUT,* drumming
its fingers, demanding discipline, why does this singer

turn up, ringing like a xylophone of gold? Tears
assault me—like my father's that he brushed away
as the bus to college gaped to swallow me. *I didn't
cry.* The Legions of Good Sense and Industriousness
plugged my eyes when they burned my childhood,

crucified its pleasures, and salted the earth. Now
that salt's washing away as sound shocks open
the clogged springs. A bumper crop of corn leaps up:
long green leaves weeping in the wind, ears swelling huge,
each kernel sweet and bursting with the woman's song.

Places I Spent One Night

Thanks to all motels, hotels, and couches-at-a-friend's
where, nearly comatose, I collapsed to sleep—
but also to the places where I thrashed all night: bed

too hard, sheets too scratchy, day ahead too jangling.
Thanks to the roofs that once kept snow from freezing me.
I understand how kings could feel, of any site that saw

their bathroom acts and heard them snore: "It's mine."
Walls that enclosed me, closets that shooed wrinkles
from my shirts, drawers that caressed my underwear,

floor that supported me, I won't forget you. Porches
I was too rushed, oak paneling I was too tired to enjoy,
garages that never got to show their stuff—I'm sorry

that I had to go. *Rules of the House* taped to the purring
Frigidaire that could have cooled ice cream I never got to eat
on place mats hand-painted with thunderbird motifs—

framed prints of mountains, seascapes, sweet Strawberry
Creek—we'd have spent more time together; but business
tugged me like a gut-hooked fish. Thanks, barbecues

I didn't light, ready to flame up and grill a perfect steak.
Thanks, driveways I'll never back out of again,
swimming pools I came too late to try, couches that sagged

in the middle or to one side, mismatched coat-hangers,
and always one locked door, hiding who knows what
skeletons, pirate doubloons, or universes where my doubles

lounge on redwood porches, charcoaling thick steaks
and staring out at yet-to-be-experienced worlds where Time's
fist—clenched so tight in this world—opens wide.

Bed & Breakfast

CALM, HAPPY, VACATION, RELAXATION, FUN ☺

> According to Apache legend, when the first man wakened to dis-
> cover the first woman beside him . . . he laughed. Then she laughed.
> And as they went off together, the world burst into springtime and
> song.
>
> —*The Death of Comedy*, Erich Segal

Funny how you've wound up in the same bed with me.
I laugh, you laugh that we, who want our son
to dress himself, love to be undressed like little kids.

I laugh, you laugh because belts, buttons, bras,
and boxers start with *b*, and are such entertaining things.
I laugh, you laugh to see how different bodies are.

We could be playing doctor, stifling giggles so parents
won't hear. I laugh, you laugh to think how
people name our favorite parts to curse—how children

get time-outs and worse for saying what we love to do.
I laugh, you laugh because, outside, a big gray squirrel,
blue jays, and acorn woodpeckers are laughing too.

I laugh, you laugh at how the squirrel's laugh sounds
like choked-back tears. We could weep for pure relief.
I laugh, you laugh to think how long we've waited,

how tortured were the roads that meet inside
this room. I laugh, you laugh to hear boys shouting,
"Easy out!" and "Dude, you're doomed!"

Hilarious, how people turn double plays, twitch
Hula Poppers, peddle cheese planes with no thought
of you and me. I laugh, you laugh to feel the fire

we make by rubbing limbs. Beyond this bed, polar
winds groan. Clouds swell to the brink of tears.
I laugh, you laugh, it's such good luck that's brought us here.

I laugh, you laugh; the whole house sings.
I laugh, you laugh. Winter's gray water-balloon bursts.
We're bathed in spring.

What Things Are Made Of

Thales thought, *Water:* nicer stuff than Alchemy's
sulfur, mercury, earth, salt, and phlegm—
although if *nice* makes *right,* Aristotle

with his earth-air-water-fire is your man.
Democritus said things are made of *atoms,*
which he thought were indivisible, but we think

are made of *quarks,* which may themselves
be made of strings, but not the kite kind,
or what make the Brahms concerto sing—theoretical

strings strummed in dimensions we can know
only by Math, which summed the universe from nothing,
Pythagoras believed, a child's face being a complex

of numbers, like photos we e-mail to friends.
Tests show the urban myth "Life weighs twenty-one
grams," is a heavy load of crap: precisely

what the world is made of, my mind insists some days.
The "problem of minds" obsessed the ancients,
as it does me, now that I'm older, hoping to hold onto mine.

How can a thing bouncy and bright as thought
vanish when a pump in my chest quits? How can anger
at a parking ticket, or joy to find a cowrie grazing

a tide pool, turn to mercury, sulfur, earth, water,
and phlegm because a clot obstructs one artery?
Minds are weightless, Descartes said: *res cogitans*

as opposed to *res extensa. Thinking* v. *extended* "stuff."
Incorporeal v. corporeal. What does God weigh?
Nothing, since He's the Ultimate *res cogitans.*

Everything, since He has no limits—*res extensa* to the max—
and everything grew out of Him. Is God water?
I've thought so on a hot day. (Lack of what substance

gave Death Valley its name?) Is Death a substance?
In the case of cyanide or a bullet to the brain,
it seems to be. It weighs me down to think of it.

And how about sadness? Love? And time? Is God
love? Is love all we need, as the Beatles sang eons ago?
When my dad died, all love felt sucked out of the room,

as if I were one of those spiders, rats, and cats Robert Hooke
killed, to the applause of London crowds, by pumping air
out of their jars, proving the existence of vacuums,

which Aristotle and Descartes denied, as did Mom's mom,
who cleaned everything by broom (corporeal), or hand—
corporeal too, and time-limited, so I suggest you take

your child's whenever he/she offers it, and love
its *res extensa,* and the weight of love that warms its flesh.
This offer is too good to last long.

ACKNOWLEDGMENTS

The author would like to thank the editors of the following publications for first publishing these poems, sometimes with other titles and in other versions:

5 AM: "Lingerie Show," "Day Before Memorial Day," "I Might as Well Have Begged a Cyclone Not to Spin," "Trouble with the Law"; *Ascent*: "The Last Bobcat"; *Asheville Poetry Review*: "Never Too Late"; *Atlanta Review*: "Bimbo Limbo"; *Bat City Review*: "Brain Silos"; *Birmingham Review*: "Sad for the Hunchback"; *Chautauqua Literary Journal*: "One Week Until Opening Day"; *Cimarron Review*: "News of Him"; *Crab Orchard Review*: "Manpanzee," "Worry Won't Help"; *Epoch*: "Nostalgia's Not What It Used to Be"; *Evansville Review*: "Vitus & Me"; *Free Lunch*: "Summer of Love"; *Gettysburg Review*: "Dark Penguin"; *Green Mountains Review*: "Nuh-Nuh-Nuh-Nuh-Nuh-Nuh-Nuh-Nuh-Nuh *Dah* Dah Dah! Doesn't Look Like Much in Print," "Where Does Joy Come In?"; *Gulf Stream*: "It Had to Do with Candy Sanders:"; *Iowa Review*: "Corn"; *Los Angeles Review*: "Man Stuck in Spiderweb," "Places I Spent One Night"; *Margie Review*: "Catfish"; *Michigan Quarterly Review*: "What Things Are Made Of"; *New Letters*: "We Could've Been Commandos"; *New Ohio Review*: "Dismantled for Goodwill, Our Son's Crib," "Don' Like"; *North American Review*: "Duck Tape"; *Paris Review*: "Sand Fish"; *Passages North*: "Handling a Trophy Trout"; *Ploughshares*: "What Kitty Knows"; *Poems & Plays*: "Nerves of Titanium"; *Poet Lore*: "On Castle Creek"; *Prairie Schooner*: "The Best Moment of My Life"; *Red Cedar Review*: "The Deed"; *Red Rock Review*: "Karen, Lost," "Without a Paddle"; *River Styx*: "Marco Polo"; *Roger*: "Where Are You Now, Sally Woodman,"; *Slate*: "Mummies to Burn," "The Sound That Wakes Me at Night, Thinking of It"; *Southern Poetry Review*: "Word of Mouth"; *Sou'wester*: "At Lamaze"; *Spillway*: "Liar's Ball"; *Sycamore Review*: "Morning Dance"; *TriQuarterly*: "Everybody Tries So Hard," "Jackass: The Viewer"; *West Branch*: "Bed & Breakfast"

The writing of this book was partially funded by California State University, Long Beach, Scholarly and Creative Activities Awards.

Special thanks to, alphabetically, Ron Koertge, Ed Ochester, Karen Schneider, and William Trowbridge for invaluable editorial assistance and to Edward Hirsch, who got the train on track.